The World of Mythology:

South Pacific Mythology

By Jim Ollhoff

Published by ABDO Publishing Company, 8000 West 78th Street, Suite 310, Edina, MN 55439. Copyright ©2012 by Abdo Consulting Group, Inc. International copyrights reserved in all countries. No part of this book may be reproduced in any form without written permission from the publisher. ABDO & Daughters™ is a trademark and logo of ABDO Publishing Company.

Printed in the United States of America, North Mankato, Minnesota.
012011
092011

 PRINTED ON RECYCLED PAPER

Editor: John Hamilton
Graphic Design: Sue Hamilton
Cover Design: Neil Klinepier
Cover Photo: Gonzalo Ordóñez
Interior Photos & Illustrations: Alamy-pg 14; AP-pg 10; Corbis-pgs 7, 15, 16, 17, 25 & 28; ESA-pg 18; Richard & Jo deMeester-pg 24; Getty Images-pgs 4, 6, 13 & 19; Glow Images-pgs 12, 21 & 30; Granger Collection-pg 11; Greta Hendrickson-pg 27; iStockphoto-pgs 30 & 31; Library of Congress-pg 9; NGA-pg 8; National Geographic-pg 23; OCHA-pg 32 (top); PNAS-pg 32 (bottom); Thinkstock-pgs 5, 24, 25, & 29

Library of Congress Cataloging-in-Publication Data

Ollhoff, Jim, 1959-
  South Pacific mythology / Jim Ollhoff.
    p. cm. -- (The world of mythology)
  ISBN 978-1-61714-727-2
  1. Legends--Oceania. 2. Mythology, Oceanian. 3. Creation--Mythology. I. Title.
  GR380.O55 2011
  398.209164'8--dc22
                          2010044266

CONTENTS

THE MIGHTY MYTH

In the 1800s, scientists believed that myths were the opposite of science. They thought that since ancient peoples didn't know why it rained, they made up stories about the rain gods. The ancients didn't understand why earthquakes happened, so they invented stories about angry earthquake gods. Those scientists in the 1800s said that because we have science today, we no longer need myths.

However, that's not a very good understanding of myths. The idea that myths explained rain and earthquakes presents only a small piece of their importance.

Myths gave people meaning before science could, but science and mythology sometimes play similar roles. Both science and mythology can help us see beyond where we are. Both science and myths can give us understanding and guidance to live in the world.

A myth is a story that is important to people. Myths tell us how to act and how to survive when times are tough. Some myths inspire us to greater courage or seek deeper knowledge.

Some myths inspire us to seek deeper knowledge.

For the people of the South Pacific Islands, myths were their connection to the gods and their ancestors.

The original people in Australia, sometimes called indigenous peoples or Aboriginals, had a myth called Dreamtime. Before anything existed, there was Dreamtime, when Life was sleeping beneath the surface of the Earth. The ancestors broke the ground, waking up Life. The sun came up out of the ground, and then the ancestors shaped the mountains, rivers, plants, animals, and people. When the ancestors were done creating, they went to sleep. Their spirits are still present in the mountains, rivers, plants, and everywhere else in the landscape. Sacred rituals reconnected the Aboriginals to the spirits of Life.

For the people of the South Pacific Islands, myths weren't just something that happened long ago. The stories were part of who they were. Myths were their connection to the gods and their ancestors. The people of the South Pacific, just like us, still use myths and stories to help us live out our lives.

Australia's Aboriginals believed the spirits of Dreamtime were present everywhere.

Above: According to the Dreamtime myth, Life was awakened by the ancestors.

THE SOUTH PACIFIC

The South Pacific, also called Oceania, is sometimes sorted into four areas: Australasia, which includes Australia and its territories, plus New Zealand; Melanesia, a group of islands to the north and west of Australia, including the islands of New Guinea, Fiji, and the Solomons; Micronesia, which includes the islands to the north of Melanesia, such as Guam and the Marshall Islands; and Polynesia, which is a triangle with corners at New Zealand, Easter Island, and Hawaii. While Hawaii is not technically in the South Pacific, its first inhabitants were from the South Pacific Islands.

Historians believe the first people to arrive in Australia came from Southeast Asia at least 40,000 years ago. Some historians think they came to Australia 65,000 years ago or earlier. People probably walked to Australia when the sea levels were much lower, or took short island hops on boats. Over the years, people took boats to live on hundreds of islands all across the South Pacific.

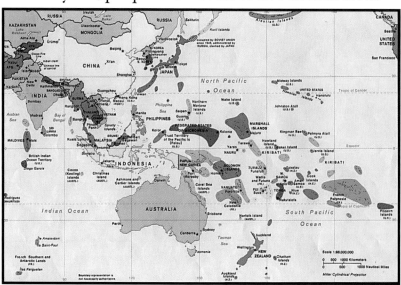

Right: The South Pacific is also known as Oceania.

Above: Historians believe that the first people to arrive on various South Pacific islands either walked when water levels were very low or used small boats.

THE SOUL OF THE SOUTH PACIFIC PEOPLES

In most of the South Pacific, early people lived in small groups of related families called clans. These clans spent their lives moving together, living together, and telling stories. Each clan had its own stories and myths. Throughout most of the South Pacific, it is rare to find myths that are told by all people.

Right: Most South Pacific people lived in small family groups called clans.

In Polynesia, however, there are more common myths, since the same group populated many of the islands there. As the Polynesians moved, they took their myths with them. The clans passed down their myths by word of mouth. Sadly, the original languages are disappearing. As the languages disappear, so do the myths. When the first Europeans came to Australia in the late 1700s, there were about 200 languages among the Aboriginals. Today, only about 50 still exist.

Many of the myths of the South Pacific were about individual heroes who took great journeys. Many of the myths reminded people to welcome others coming from the sea. These stories probably stretched back to a time when their ancestors really had to take great journeys across the sea.

Above: When the first Europeans came to the South Pacific, most natives welcomed them. Native myths told of heroes who took great journeys across the sea.

Australia: The Rainbow Snake

Many of the Aboriginal tribes of Australia lived in deserts, and several of their myths are about the search for water. One common story, which has many versions, describes a boy walking through the desert. The boy looked for water, but could not find any. The sun got hotter and hotter, and the boy grew more and more thirsty.

Then, he saw a giant snake winding across the landscape. Behind the snake, a river emerged. As the snake slithered, it formed gorges full of gushing water, and the boy could finally quench his thirst. The snake had different names, depending on the tribe telling the story. Sometimes it was called the Rainbow Snake.

The Rainbow Snake was a protector of people. In some versions, it fought with the sun, who tried to dry up the water.

An Aboriginal rock painting of the Rainbow Snake in Australia.

Above: A Rainbow Snake costumed character entertains people at a rugby game between Australia and New Zealand. The Rainbow Snake was a protector of people.

AUSTRALIA: THE WAWILAK SISTERS

During Dreamtime, the time before the world was completely created, the two Wawilak sisters walked along the ocean. One carried a baby, and the other was pregnant. As they walked along the ocean, they named the animals and plants. They each carried a spear, and hunted animals and ate plants to survive. They finally came to rest near a lake. However, they didn't realize that the powerful Rainbow Snake was sleeping in the lake, under the surface of the water.

The Rainbow Snake awoke because of the noisy sisters, and became very angry. He was so angry that he swallowed them whole.

One version of the story says that the sisters transformed in the Rainbow Snake's stomach. Another version of the story says that the other snakes began to wonder what happened to the sisters. They kept questioning the Rainbow Snake. Finally, the wind came and battered the Rainbow Snake until he vomited up the sisters.

One of the deeper meanings of this myth is to remind people that both women (represented by the sisters) and men (represented by the male Rainbow Snake) need each other, and both genders should be respected and honored. Among the Yolngu, this myth is still recited in traditional ceremonies where boys become official members of the tribe.

Above: An Australian Aboriginal man and woman. The myth of the Wawilak sisters is a reminder that women (represented by the sisters) and men (represented by the male Rainbow Snake) need each other.

AUSTRALIA: THE CREATION OF HUMANS

Many Aboriginal tribes had no separate stories telling about the creation of humans. They saw themselves as part of nature—one piece of nature's giant puzzle. So, humans were created at the same time as plants, kangaroos, rivers, and everything else.

But there is one story that explains human creation. Two brothers, the Ungambikula, created themselves from nothingness. They looked around the Earth and saw many half-created plants and animals that had begun to rise from the life in the soil. The Ungambikula brothers saw creatures without eyes or ears, with arms and legs only half emerged from the mud. The brothers felt sorry for these human creatures, and so they used knives to cut the humans from the mud. They gave the humans eyes, ears, and the will to make choices.

An Aboriginal man tells his son the stories of their tribe.

Above: Two brothers, the Ungambikula, helped humans emerge from the mud.

Australia: Spirits, Spirits, Everywhere

ustralian Aboriginal tribes believed that the ancient gods left parts of themselves everywhere. Therefore, every place, every tree, every rock, and every animal has a sacred godliness to it.

One myth tells the story of a great tribal chief named Mululu. He knew that his death was approaching, and he knew that he would miss his daughters when he was dead. He asked if they would join him in the sky. He told them to seek out a certain shaman, a person who communicates with the spirit world. This shaman had the longest beard in the world, and he would help them reunite after Mululu's death.

Sure enough, Mululu died, and his daughters sought the bearded shaman. They found him, a man whose beard went on forever. He braided his beard, and the daughters climbed it into the heavens. The sisters formed the constellation that we call the Southern Cross. Mululu became the star we call Alpha Centauri, one of the closest stars to Earth.

Above: One Aboriginal myth tells the story of a great chief named Mululu, who knew he was dying. He asked his daughters to talk to a shaman who would help the family reunite.

New Zealand: Creation of the Universe

The Maori were a Polynesian people who settled in New Zealand before 1300 AD. The Maori myth of creation began with a terrible nothingness. Two beings emerged from the nothingness: Rangi, the male sky god, and Papa, the Earth goddess. They embraced, holding each other tight like an oyster shell. They eventually gave birth to six children—the gods of the sea, plants, forests, and elements. But the space between Rangi and Papa was so tight that there was little air to breath, and the children couldn't even stand.

At one point, Papa raised her arm briefly. This allowed the children to see the sunlight—and they liked it. The children tried to pry Rangi and Papa apart. Finally, they were successful. They got Rangi and Papa separated and used wooden poles to keep Rangi suspended over Papa. This separation caused Rangi and Papa great grief. Raindrops are the tears of Rangi, and the fog and dew are the tears of Papa.

Right: Maori myth says the fog and dew are the tears of Papa, the Earth goddess.

Above: The Maori of New Zealand tell the creation story of Rangi, the male sky god, and Papa, the Earth goddess. As the first two beings, they became the parents of all things.

New Zealand: The Origin of Suffering

New Zealand is home to the good god Io, who had three baskets of wisdom. The first basket contained all the knowledge of peace and love. The second basket contained the knowledge of religion. The third basket contained the knowledge of survival. Io wanted to share this knowledge with all the humans. Io chose the god Tane for the very important job of sharing the wisdom with humanity.

Tane took the baskets and began spreading the wisdom all over Polynesia. However, the evil god Whiro was insanely jealous. Whiro wanted to be the one to share the knowledge with people. He was so angry that he sent centipedes, ants, spiders, and other creatures to stop Tane. There was a giant battle, and Tane was victorious. Whiro was confined to the underworld. However, the suffering that Whiro unleashed stayed in the world. Since then, there has always been suffering, disease, and death in the world.

Right: A New Zealand weta. It was said that the evil god Whiro sent all types of creatures to stop the god Tane from sharing wisdom with humanity.

Above: A Maori tribesman in a New Zealand forest. According to myth, the forest god Tane was chosen to give wisdom to Polynesians.

New Zealand: The Origin of Coconut

Hina was a beautiful young woman, and she liked to lounge and bathe at a deep pool that was full of eels. Whenever she came to the pool, the eels would leave, except for one. This eel, named Tuna, would change itself into a young man whenever she came to the pool. They became friends and fell in love.

There are many versions of what happened next in this story. According to one version, Tuna came to Hina one day and told her that he could no longer see her. Tuna told her that a huge rainstorm would come, and that it would cause a terrible flood. Tuna told her that he would swim up to her as an eel, and she must cut off his head and bury it.

The rains came and created a flood, just as Tuna had predicted. Hina cut off the eel's head and buried it. Soon, tiny shoots appeared where the head had been buried. The shoots grew into coconut trees, which gave food and milk. Coconut shells made bowls, and the strands of fiber were used as rope for building houses and canoes.

The Maori say that when the husk of a coconut is removed, the eyes and mouth of an eel are still visible.

A freshwater eel in New Zealand.

A coconut tree sprouts and grows. Coconuts were a vital resource for the native peoples of New Zealand.

POLYNESIA: MAUI, THE TRICKSTER

Almost every culture's mythology included at least one trickster. The trickster was a mischievous god who played tricks and often got into trouble. Sometimes he did good things, but sometimes he was too clever for his own good. For the Polynesians, Maui was a trickster and a hero. Maui today is the name of one of the Hawaiian Islands.

There are many stories about Maui. He was said to be born nearly dead, and so he was thrown into the ocean. He was revived by the sun god.

One story tells how people needed more time each day to tend their crops and cook their meals. So, Maui made a net with his sister's hair and ensnared the sun, delaying it as it moved across the sky.

Another story tells how Maui brought fire to humans. He went to find the goddess Mahui-ike, whose fingernails were always on fire. He tricked her into giving fire to the humans.

Another Maui myth tells how he and his brothers were out fishing, and when he fell asleep, his bait caught something huge. When he finally pulled his catch to the surface, he realized it wasn't a fish at all. It was the North Island of New Zealand.

Right: Maui was said to have tricked the goddess Mahui-ike into giving fire to humans.

Above: Maui snared the sun to delay it from moving across the sky.

HAWAII: PELE, THE VOLCANO GODDESS

Volcanoes on the islands of Hawaii can roar with a terrible rage at a moment's notice. The Polynesians believed that Pele, the goddess of volcanoes and fire, had a terrible temper.

Some versions of the Pele myth say that Pele was always fighting with her sister. To separate them, their father exiled Pele to Hawaii. While she was building a fire pit on one of the Hawaiian Islands, Pele was attacked by her sister and left for dead. When she recovered, she went to the other Hawaiian Islands and built fire pits there.

Before she died, Pele built a fire pit for herself on Kilauea, an active volcano on today's island of Hawaii. After she died, she became a goddess. When a Hawaiian volcano erupts, it is because Pele is angry or annoyed. According to Polynesian legend, she lives in Kilauea Volcano to this day.

Right: An islander chanting to Pele, the goddess of volcanoes and fire.

Above: According to myth, Pele built fire pits on the Hawaiian Islands. Before she died, she built one for herself, today's Kilauea, on the island of Hawaii.

GLOSSARY

An Australian Aboriginal man.

A Maori warrior with traditional facial tattoos. His expression is meant to scare his enemies.

ABORIGINALS
The tribal people that have been in Australia for tens of thousands of years.

AUSTRALASIA
An area that includes Australia and its territories, plus New Zealand.

DREAMTIME
A time when the world was created according to Australian aboriginal myth.

MAORI
A Polynesian people who settled in New Zealand before 1300 AD.

MELANESIA
A group of islands to the north and west of Australia, including the islands of New Guinea, Fiji, and the Solomons.

MICRONESIA

An area that includes the islands to the north of Melanesia, such as Guam and the Marshall Islands.

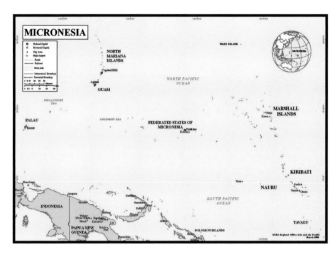

PAPA

Also known as Papatuanuku. In Maori mythology, Papa was the Earth mother or goddess of the Earth. Her partner was Rangi, the sky father or god of the sky.

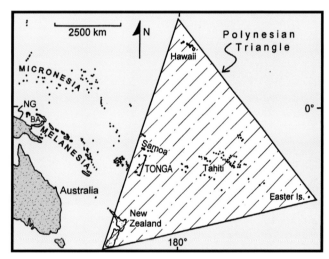

POLYNESIA

A triangular area with corners at New Zealand, Easter Island, and Hawaii.

RANGI

Also known as Ranginui. In Maori mythology, Rangi was the sky father or god of the sky. His partner was Papa, the Earth mother or goddess of the Earth.

SHAMAN

A person in a tribe who could communicate with the spirit world. A religious leader or healer.

INDEX